# THE GREAT ALASKAN BACHELOR'S COOKBOOK

### By

### BOB B MULLER

"Junk Food Cooking At It's Finest"

Just throw a bunch of junk together and cook it

No Fret - No Sweat

No Pain - No Strain

- - - - - - - - - - - - - - - - - - - - - - -

Quick easy ways to cook good meals
Even if you don't know how to cook

- - - - - - - - - - - - - - - - - - - - - - -

Written for bachelors by a bachelor

(Girls have my permission to
use these recipes also)

ISBN: 978-1-4269-3470-4 (sc)

ISBN: 978-1-4269-3471-1 (e-book)

*Our mission is to efficiently provide the world's finest, most comprehensive book publishing service, enabling every author to experience success. To find out how to publish your book, your way, and have it available worldwide, visit us online at www.trafford.com*

*Trafford rev. 6/23/2010*

 www.trafford.com

North America & international
toll-free: 1 888 232 4444 (USA & Canada)
phone: 250 383 6864 ♦ fax: 812 355 4082

Created and Written by the Bachelor
ROBERT B MULLER
Author


Illustrated by the Gorgeous
Judith Ann Crampton
Illustrator


Proofed by the Beautiful
Brandi Nelson
Proof Reader

## THE NOTHING PAGE

This is the "NOTHING" page. There's nothing on it.
(It just makes you wonder what happens next!!!)

## DEDICATION

This book is dedicated to my father, Robert D
Muller, the finest cook I have ever known.

To my younger brother, Richard, whose cooking is
second only to Dad.

And to the world's bachelors and bachelorettes
in hopes that these recipes will help them attract
their desired sweethearts without having to attend
cooking schools and having to exert only a minimal
effort in the kitchen.

# INTRODUCTION

To the World:

My first cooking experience was at age 4 when Mom called me to breakfast and I boldly announced that I would cook my own when I was ready. Mom agreed and smilingly watched my first attempt to cook a hard boiled egg in a little pan from a toy cooking set on our flat top oil stove. After that failure, I always went to eat when Mom called

Living in Alaska, I eventually became a campfire cook: Cutting potatoes, carrots, onions, and meat into a cast iron skillet with a little oil or water and fryng them over a campfire. Mom taught me to roast food in an oven and I learned to fry eggs, pancakes, and french toast. Tasty - but nothing fancy.

I viewed cooking as I did school homework — time consuming. Time could better be spent playing Chess, working on cars, or serenading a girl friend.

I haven't changed much. But I sometimes get the urge to cook. Usually to impress a lady or because I get a particular taste for something.

My bachelor days taught me quick cooking. The bare essentials, but tastes good and keeps you alive.

Ladies make a real production out of cooking and after a bit of time they produce really good stuff, like Pizza Fondue or Lasagna. Me, I just throw a bunch of stuff together and let the stove do the work. Sometimes I really surprize myself with something exceptionally good.

As I progressed, I wrote the successful recipes in a blank page book. So here they are for guys who want to impress thier ladies. You just need food, a stove, some cooking utensils, a girl to impress, and very little luck.

So, Have at it!!!

*Robert B mully*

VI

# FOREWORD

I cooked these recipes using an electric stove.

If you use a gas stove, you will have to experiment a little with the size of the flame and the timing might be a little different for broiling and boiling. Baking or roasting in the oven will have the same timing since the oven is temperature regulated. A damp atmostphere will change the timing somewhat also. I cook in Alaska where the air is fairly dry.

When broiling in an electric stove, place the tray about six inches beneath the broiling element. (Usually the second notch down as shown.)

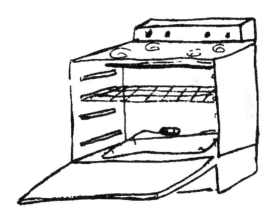

# TABLE OF CONTENTS

xl

## MEET RALPH!!

I'm Ralph. (Girls may call me Ralphie.)
I love Girls! I love life! I'm a bachelor bird
and I've agreed to explain this book for
Bob

## MEET HERBY

I'm Herby. And Ralph is
helpless without me. I'm
the world's greatest taster
and cooking critic.

1

Before reading any further: **Follow the following instructions**

Put together on your counter the following items:

1. One baking dish with a glass top
2. 4 potatoes, each the size of your fist
3. Two pork chops
4. One cup of flour
5. 1 package of sliced American Cheese
6. One big onion, the size of your fist
7. One cube of butter
8. One gallon of milk
9. The following seasonings: salt, rubbed dalmation sage, ground black pepper, and paprika

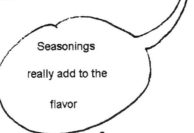

Seasonings really add to the flavor

2

Fill the bowl like the picture shows

cheese slices
onion chunks
sage everywhere
potato slices
pork chop

Mix two or three heaping Tablespoons of flour in
3 cups of cold milk in a blender and pour into the bowl.

If you need more liquid to cover the top, add more milk.

BAKING DISH
WITH
GLASS TOP

OVEN
RACK

COOKIE SHEET UNDER BAKING DISH

Close the oven door. Set timer for 1 1/2 hours.

Now sit back and read this book until the timer goes off. When the timer goes off, you may turn off the oven, remove the baking dish with hot pan holders and eat.

You have just cooked your first dinner while reading this book.

## SAFETY FIRST !!!

### Do not smoke in any kitchen - NOT EVER !!!

Wear an apron for protection against food stains and hot food burns. YOU'RE A SLOB, JUST LIKE ME, and YOU WILL SPILL THINGS, JUST LIKE ME !!!

Stoves are hot. Yes, Really! So are pots and pans and metal forks and knives and spoons! So use insulating cooking gloves and hot pan holders.

Stir with wooden spoons. They don't get too hot, they don't scratch pans, and they clean easily.

Always keep your knives sharp. Dull knives cause you to bear down too hard when trying to cut - then they slip and cut you.

Never make sudden moves when holding utensils - because you might cut someone else.

If you drop a knife, don't try to catch it and don't scream. Just step quickly out of it's way and let it fall.

Remember that cooking food causes steam. So when you lift a lid off a pan, do it as the picture shows, so you won't scald your wing.

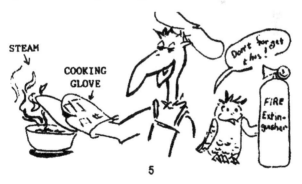

STEAM

COOKING GLOVE

Don't forget this!

FIRE Extin-guisher

5

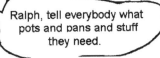

Ralph, tell everybody what
pots and pans and stuff
they need.

Right on, Herby.
There are some basic
things you need.

1. A large knife to cut, slice, and
   chop 8 to 12 inches long.
2. A small paring knife to peel
   with a 3 to 4 inch blade

3. A 12 inch diameter frying pan
   and a spatula. (A glass lid for the
   pan is nice also.)

4. A large wooden spoon.
5. A one quart pan with a lid.
6. A 2 quart pan with a lid.
7. A 5 quart pan with a lid.
8. A flat cookie sheet.
9. A set of plastic measuring cups.
10. A set of measuring spoons.

(Non stick pans are good for
beginners, although I prefer
Stainless steel. Glass lids are
preferable to metal lids.)

6

7

And now for special statements after which we will begin cooking:

Never, ever, peel a potato. Wash it, cut out bad spots, but don't peel it. The flavor is in the peeling. Even for mashed potatoes.

"Doubts" approach me. I'm beginning to think he's losing his mind.

8

9

10

## DINNERS

First, we're going to cook some dinners. For several reasons.

1. You normally have your Lady-bird friend over for dinner long before she comes for lunch or breakfast.
2. What you cook for dinner can also be used for lunches.
3. Dinner leftovers are great for next day for meals and snacks.

OH, BROTHER! Dig him! Listen to Casanova, the Great Alaskan Lover Cook. This I gotta see.

11

## ROAST RUMP DINNER

Place the following items on you
counter top:

4 pounds rump roast
8 fist size potatoes - each cut into 4
    pieces
8 carrots
8 golf ball sized onions
1 head of cabbage cut into 12 large
    chunks

Put roast in the roast pan and scatter
the veggies all around it. Sprinkle
some sage, garlic salt, and pepper
over everything.

**ROAST PAN**

(Continued on next page)

Stick a knife into the roast. Remove it and stick the meat thermometer into the hole. Pour in two cups water, put the top on and put it in the oven. Turn the oven to "bake" at 350 degrees.
Set your timer for one hour. That's when you first check the thermometer. Open the oven door and check the thermometer once in awhile. When it reads 150 degrees, the roast is done.
Turn the oven off first, then remove the roast from the oven.

Roast

Turn the oven off
and eat it. (The
food , that is.)

Gravy on next page. For salad and salad dressing, turn to pages 17-23 and 42.

The following recipe will be made after the roast is cooked, but read it over now.

## LUMPLESS GRAVY

Take 8 chunks of potatoes, 1 onion and 1 carrot from the roast pan and drop into a blender. Add 1 teaspoon ground black pepper.

Cover them with juice from the roast. Turn the blender on until the stuff turns into goup, like axle grease.

Pour the goup into pan and add the rest of the juice from the roast pan in with the goup. Heat at medium heat while stirring. It takes only a few minutes and there is your gravy.

15

The roast is now in the oven cooking.
This is a good time to set the table. (If you don't
have wine, then place a Rose or a Carnation in a
glass with water and a teaspoon of sugar - it's not
for drinking - it sets a romantic atmostphere.)

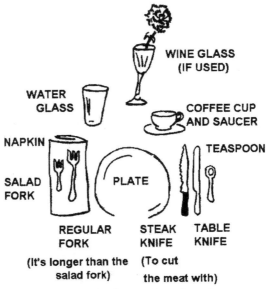

WINE GLASS
(IF USED)

WATER
GLASS

COFFEE CUP
AND SAUCER

NAPKIN

TEASPOON

SALAD
FORK

PLATE

REGULAR         STEAK      TABLE
FORK            KNIFE      KNIFE

(It's longer than the   (To cut
salad fork)          the meat with)

One setting for your lovely sweetie and one for you.
(Your own setting does not need a flower.)

**NOW BUILD YOUR SALAD**

16

Salad is the easiest thing in the world to make.

A good salad for a beginner is just half a head of lettuce, 2 large tomatoes, and one cucumber.

It's a little tastier if you also add one bell pepper (any color) and 3 sticks of celery.

You cut and mix the ingredients together.
How you cut them is about to be explained.

17

## LETTUCE

One of the best ways is to rip half-a-head of
lettuce apart with your CLEAN bare hands.
Then tear it into golf ball size chunks with your
fingers and throw the chunks into a large bowl.

A second way is to shred it through a meat
grinder or, three, slice it crosswise as shown.
After slicing it you can easily pull it apart and
throw into your salad bowl.

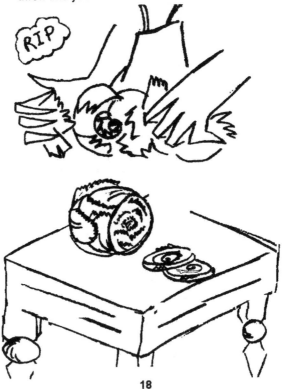

## CUCUMBERS

You can use them peeled or not peeled.
(Most people like them peeled)

The easiest way to peel them is to cut them
as shown into several pieces.

**end pieces**

Then with a paring knife, peel it like this:

Be careful you don't cut yourself. Then slice it
as shown below and put the pieces in the salad
bowl.

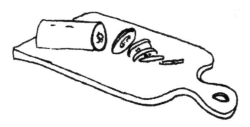

19

**Tomatoes can be cut three basic ways**

Lengthwise like little canoes or like
pieces of an orange

crosswise into thin slices or

chunked.  Cut crosswise and lengthwise
into random size chunks.

Use any of the above ways and throw
the pieces into a bowl with lettuce.

## GREEN PEPPERS

Cut them in half, then clean out the core and the seeds with a table spoon and your fingers.

Then you can cut the shell into odd sized chunks or long pieces.

Usually, you will want to cut it in small chunks the size of your fingernail when putting it in a salad.

Slicing it in long thin pieces then cutting the pieces crosswise gives good chunks.

Throw the chunks into the bowl with the lettuce, tomatoes, and cucumbers.

## CELERY

TRIM
OFF

Cut the stalk into bite size chunks as shown:

**DON'T USE THE TOPS**

Throw the chunks into the bowl with the lettuce, tomatoes, cucumbers, and bell peppers.

Now mix the stuff up with your CLEAN hands.

Yor salad is now ready.

For your salad dressing, go to the next page.

NOTE: Leftover salad can be blended in the blender and used in soup. Do this instead of throwing it out.

LARGE FORK                    LARGE SPOON

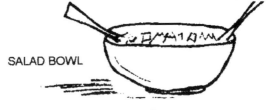

SALAD BOWL

22

# YOUR FIRST SALAD DRESSING

In a bowl, pour:

1/4 cup white distilled vinegar
1/2 cup tomato catsup
1/4 teaspoon oregano seasoning
1/4 teaspoon celery seed seasoning
1/8 teaspoon dill weed seasoning
1 Tablespoon mayonnaise

Mix well with a spoon or dump in a blender and blend for 30 seconds.

It's ready. Put it on the table in a bowl with a spoon or be real impressive and buy a salad dressing vase like the one at the bottom of the page.

 Plastic or glass (available in most grocery stores) - - - pour the salad dressing in it and put it on the table.

23

When through with all the salad and dressing, put it on the table, clean the kitchen, and go swoon over your girlfriend while the roast is cooking. When it is ready, your timer or alarm clock will tell you, (if you remembered to set it). Then slice the meat crosswise across the grain in 1/2 inch thick slices. Put the meat on a plate. Put all the veggies in a big bowl with a large spoon, and put everything on the table.

A couple of candles (LIT) would be nice and soft music

### - - - NOT ROCK !!! - - -

Now, seat the lady at the table and eat dinner. (It impresses ladies if you offer to serve them!)

**Tomorrow, you can take the leftovers
and make an excellent soup.**

1. Throw all the salad into a blender and blend it into a goupy mush.

2. Cut all the left over veggies into chunks the size of your thumbtips.

3. Cut 1/2 of the leftover meat into large marble sizes chunks. (Save the other half to slice for sandwiches).

4. Mix everything together in a pan with enough water to cover everything.

5. Pour in the leftover gravy.

6. Cook over medium heat while stirring, until hot.   Now    PIG OUT!!!

## DINNERS

You'll find that meat and potatoes take the longest to cook. So you can get them cooking and while they are, you can put vegetables on the stove to cook. Then you can make salad, salad dressing, and other side dishes and set the table. If you're real ambitious (and smart) you'll also use this time to clean up your mess in the kitchen. (Including dirty dishes).

- - - - - - - - - - - - - - - -

If you want to buy meat on sale, and freeze it, here is a little more on the subject - - - -

## FROZEN MEATS

I can't say how the experts do it, but when I wrap meat to freeze, I use white freezer paper (wax on one side),tape it shut with masking tape, and write the weight, kind of meat, and date on the package. (Sometimes the price per pound also, to compare future prices)

When wrapping more than one piece in the same wrap, I separate the pieces with a piece of freezer wrap paper.

This way I can separate pieces, while still frozen, by prying them apart with a large knife. To remove any paper that is frozen to the meat, just run hot water over it for a few seconds and the paper will easily come off.

Thaw meat in the refrigerator, use a thaw (Defrost) setting on a microwave or other oven or put in a container and cover completely with water and cover the container. These methods help prevent food poisoning bacteria to grow on the food.

## FILET MIGNON, NEW YORK, OR SIRLOIN TIP STEAK
## BROILED FROZEN

Buy a whole Filet Mignon, New York, or Sirloin Tip and cut it into 4 to 8 ounce steaks each 1 1/2 thick. They will come about 6 inches long and 2 1/2 inches wide each. Wrap them, 2 together, in freezer paper, then food film and store them in the freezer.

You are now ready for unexpected guests or a quick steak dinner when you want one.

Simply remove from the freezer, run hot water over them, remove the wrappings, and pry them apart.

Now put them, still frozen, on a pan 5 inches under the broiler element and broil them for exactly 10 minutes per side, with the oven door partly open.
Toaster ovens will do the same with the door closed.

You now have a perfect medium rare steak.

While the steak is cooking, make a salad and you have dinner in 20 minutes.

## FILET MIGNON, NEW YORK STRIP, SIRLOIN STEAK
## FRIED

1" to 1 1/2 " thick steak (Thawed - not frozen)
Turn burner on high - use a cast iron skillet. Rub some butter over the skillet surface (inside, not outside). Put the steak in the skillet and fry for 2 minutes on each side.

Now fry another 2 minutes on each side a second time
Now fry another 2 minutes on each side a third time.

Now eat a really good medium rare steak

28

## PEACHY ROAST PORK LOIN

2 lb pork loin roast
1 fresh apple
1 15-ounce can of peach halves in heavy syrup

Take the pork from the freezer and place in pan in oven (still frozen). Turn oven to 450 degrees and cook for 1 1/2 hours. (After the first hour insert a meat thermometer into the roast)

Prepare the peach sauce from page 49.

Cut each peach half into 2 pieces.

Cut apple in half and remove the core. Then cut the apple halves into lengthwise slices (like canoes)

Remove the roast from oven and criss cross the top with a knife, then Toothpick the apple and peach pieces to the roast

Pour the peach sauce over the roast and fruit.

Put it back in the oven and cook for 30 more minutes. The meat thermometer should read 165 degrees.

It is ready to eat.

A bowl of apple sauce always goes good with pork, as well as pineapple slices.

30

## LARGE ROAST BEEF DINNER

Take a frozen 4 lb sirloin tip or rump roast from your freezer and place in a large roasting pan that is large enough for a small turkey. Turn your oven to 450 degrees. Add 12 small potatoes or 6 large potatoes cut in half.

Add a full stalk of celery with leaves and base cut off and with the stalk cut in half for shorter pieces.

Add 12 egg size onions or pieces cut from a big onion. Cut 2 12-inch long Zuchini squashes into 2 inch long pieces and add them to the pan.

Cut 2 bell peppers into large chunks and add them. Cut 1 lb of carrots into 3 inch pieces and add them. Stick a meat thermometer in the meat.

Scatter the veggies all around the meat and pour 2 quarts of water in the pan (enough water to cover 2/3 of the meat).

Cook without a lid at 450 degrees for 60 minutes.

Now cover the pan with a lid or aluminum foil and cook at 350 degrees for 60 more minutes.

# ROAST BEEF

(Chuck Roast, Pot Roast, Sirloin Tip Roast, Rump Roast, Rib Roast, Etc.)

They all cook about the same, 350 degrees for approximately 20 minutes per pound. (If it is thawed). It will take longer if it is frozen (20 minutes to an hour depending on how much it weighs).

For best results, use a meat thermometer. Stab a knife into the side of the thickest part of the meat, then insert the thermometer into the stab hole.

Cook the meat until you reach what you want from this chart:    (These are the temperatures in the middle of the roast)

Rare - 125 degrees
Medium Rare - 135 degrees
Medium - 145
Medium Well - 155
Well Done - 165 (A completely ruined meat and not recommended)

\*\*\* I recommend Medium Rare in the middle. The meat will be more done towards the ends of the roast. Medium half way and Well Done at the ends. Everyone will be pleased.

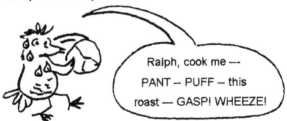

Ralph, cook me —
PANT — PUFF — this
roast — GASP! WHEEZE!

## A GOOD ROAST BEEF DINNER

4 to 5 pound roast of your choice.
Put it in a pan 3 times bigger than the roast itself.

Cut 6 potatoes into 4 pieces each. Stuff the potatoes
and 6 small onions around the meat. Sprinkle a little
sage, garlic salt, and pepper lightly over the meat and
vegetables. Pour in 1 cup of water. Put a meat
thermometer in the meat. Cover the whole mess with a
pan lid or tin foil.

Large chunks of cabbage stuffed in also makes the
meal most excellent.

Bake at 350 degrees for approximately 2 hours (until the
thermometer says 150 degrees F)

The leftovers with the juices and water make an
excellent soup. Add blended cooked potatoes for
thickness and you have a great stew.

33

## MULLER'S SPECIAL BAKED HAM

Buy a boneless - precooked ham (I used a 12
pound ham for Thanksgiving.)

Cut it lengthwise 3, 4, or 5 times, cutting about
halfway in to create gulleys, as shown below —

GULLEYS

HAM

Now mix with a spoon (in a bowl):
   2 cups applesauce
   1 cup beer
   1 Tablespoon crushed cloves

Pour the mess into the ham gulleys and all over the
ham. Bake for 1-1/2 hours in the oven and it's done.

You can also use toothpicks to stick pineapple slices
all over the ham. And if you wanna get real fancy,
stick cherries on the ends of the toothpicks.

Sometimes, I add peach and pear slices to the
toothpicks. (If you use too much, it'll look like a
fruitcake and everyone will think you are one - but it'll
still taste real good.)

## FRIED PORK CHOPS

Thaw the pork chops if they are frozen.

Wipe a capful of vegetable oil in a skillet.
Place pork chops in skillet and turn on the heat.
Cover the skillet with a lid and turn the heat to
medium high. Cook five mintes and then turn the
chops over. Cook another five minutes. Turn them
again and cook for a third five minutes. Turn again
and cook for a fourth five minutes.

Now eat them and feed them to your girl friend.

## FLOURED PORK CHOPS

Pour flour (any kind you want) on a plate about
1/2 inch deep.

Touch both sides of thawed chops to the flour so
that the flour sticks to the chops.

Fry at medium heat in a lightly oiled skillet for 8
minutes per side.

(Serve while still hot.)

Guess what?! It's potato time!! (Thrilling, isn't it?)

## BOILED POTATOES

Cover potatoes in a pan with water about 1/2 inch over the top of the potatoes. Boil for 20 minutes.

Once boiled, refrigerate. You can cut them up and fry them for breakfast. Bake them with cheese. Put them in roasts. Make potato salad with them. Or whatever. You can take one from the refrigerator and eat it, with or with out salt.
Reheat and pour sauce over it. (Tastes good with Hollandaise sauce.) Use your imagination.

IMPORTANT NOTE:

Always clean a potato with water before cooking. Always cook with the peeling on, even for mashed potatoes. Never peel a potato.

Your potatoes will always taste good if you follow this important rule.

Even if the skin looks ugly, leave it on. Cut off sprouts or spots but LEAVE THE PEELINGS ON. PERIOD. THERE ARE NO EXCEPTIONS.

Just checking to see
if you're doing
Okay

36

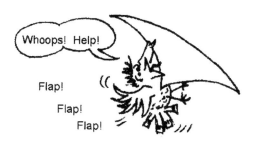

## SAGE FRIED POTATOES

Use washed but unpeeled spuds. Slice crosswise and lay in frying pan lightly oiled with bacon grease.

Cover each layer with a lot of sage, a little pepper, and a little onion salt. Cook no more than two layers at a time. Fry for a few minutes at high heat, turn over and recover with sage, pepper, and onion salt again. Fry again at high heat, then eat.

When cooking with high heat, be careful not to burn the food.

Excellent with eggs over-easy.

## BAKED POTATOES WITH CHEESE

Cut pre-boiled potato length-wise 3 times but not all the way through. Put a slice of cheese in each slit. (Use any kind of cheese you want.)

Bake at 350 degrees for 10-15 minutes (until the cheese is melted.)

Serve.

## MASHED POTATOES

Boil several potatoes for 20 minutes with the skins on, then drain off the water.

Cut them into several large pieces each and drop them back into the pan.

Now take a potato masher and take out your anxieties on the potatoes.

Mash them, beat them, smash them, and eat them. (Notice the catchy little rhyme there?)

Now don't you feel better?!?

POTATO MASHER

To make them real tasty, mash a half cube of butter in with them.

If you like them goupy, then also add 1/8 to 1/4 cup milk, or water, along with the butter.

Onion salt goes good with mashed potatoes. Some people sprinkle in ground black pepper.

Be creative - Use your imagination.

38

## - - - CAUTION - - -

If you get too carried away, however, you could
experience some drastic results. So try your creations
on yourself before force feeding your sweetie - - or
she might force feed you.

Luckily, Ralph has Herby to try them out on.

## FRENCH FRIES

Slice potatoes lengthwise into long strips. Thin or thick, with the peelings on.

Put them in a skillet. Pour in enough vegetable oil or bacon grease to barely cover the tops of the spuds (Potatoes.) Cook at high heat until golden brown.

CAUTION: If grease begins to smoke, turn heat down. Grease can catch on fire.

You must follow this important rule: Even if the skins look ugly, cut out any sprouts and spots - - -

BUT LEAVE THE SKINS (PEELINGS) ON. PERIOD. ABSOLUTELY NO EXCEPTIONS.

## VEGGIES

("vegetables" to the commoner)

## ARTICHOKES

Remove outer layer of petals and throw them away. Rinse what's left with hot water and salt, then trim off the spikes with scissors.
Place upright in pan, fill with water half way up the artichoke.
When the water is good and hot, pour butter and lemon juice into the artichoke (A little of each). Cover with a pan lid and cook for 30 minutes, barely boiling.
Remove from pan and eat.
The artichoke heart is fantastic.
Eat one petal at a time by scraping the meat off the inside of the petal by pulling it between your teeth.

## CANNED CORN

(And other canned veggies)

(I mentioned corn first because it best describes this book.)

Dump the corn into a pot. Cook over medium heat until boiling. Then another 3 minutes. It's ready.

Treat canned vegetables all the same. You can "mix and match" canned veggies together, if you want. Canned tomatoes, beats, asparagus cook the same. Tomato Soup, Paste, or Sauce can be added for additional flavor.

Corn, beets, and peas are naturally sweet and will sweeten other foods.

Some good combinations:
Beets OR tomatoes with green and/or string beans
Peas with corn and/or carrots
Corn and Green/string beans
Peas, corn and stewed tomatoes

## CORN ON THE COB

Grill unshucked corn over a barbecue grill for an hour. Shuck and eat. OR shuck the corn and place in a pot half full of water - bottom of corn on bottom of pot. Bring water to a boil the, then cook for 20 to 30 minutes.

I think corn is best by itself, but some insist on buttered corn. Melt a couple cubes of butter and pour it over the corn or, better yet, let the "butter babies" butter their own corn. Give them a cup with melted butter in it and let them ruin the corn by themselves. Rolling a cob over a plate with melted butter on it is the best way to butter it.

41

## BUILDING SALAD DRESSINGS

### ITALIAN - VINEGAR AND OIL

1/4 cup white distilled vinegar
1/2 cup vegetaable oil or olive oil
1/4 cup teaspoon oregano
1/4 teaspoon celery seed
1/4 teaspoon dill weed

Blend 30 seconds in a blender. (If you don't have one, then it's time to get one.)

### FRENCH DRESSING

Use above recipe except:
Do not use vegetable oil or olive oil.
Instead, use 1/2 cup tomato catsup or ketchup.
Blend 30 seconds.

### RUSSIAN STYLE FRENCH

Follow directions above for French Dressing.
Then, in addition, add 1/2 cup mayonaise.
Blend for 2 minutes.

### SIMPLE THOUSAND ISLAND DRESSING

Follow directions for the above Russian Style French, but also add two tablespoons of Sweet Pickle Relish and a chopped up hard boil egg.

### VARIATIONS

Italian: Use only 1/4 cup vinegar and add 1/4 cup white wine.
French, Russian Style French, or Thousand Island: Use only 1/4 cup vinegar and add 1/4 cup red wine.
For any of the dressings: Add 1/4 cup sweet or dill pickle juice.

You can build the Italian dressing first by quadrupling, (that means 4 times as much). Use 1/4 of it as Italian dressing. Take the remaining 3/4 and add 1 1/2 cups tomato catsup. Use 1/3 of the new dressing as french.

Take the remainder and add 1 cup mayonnaise. Use half of this for Russian Style French Dressing.

Take the remaining half, add two Tablespoons pickle relish and you have Thousand Island Dressing. (the Best tasting !000 Island dressing has chopped up hard boiled eggs in it. With or without the yolks, but especially the whites.)

## SWEET LIGHT FRENCH

*A never-fail recipe*
1/4 cup  white mountain chablis wine
1/4 cup vegetable oil
1/4 cup white vinegar
1 flat Tablespoon white granulated sugar

Blend 20 seconds in a blender. Serve cool. Store in refrigerator.

## RED SWEET LIGHT FRENCH

1/2 cup red burgandy wine
1/4 cup white distilled vinegar
1/2 cup tomato catsup
1 flat Tablespoon regular sugar or 2 flat
    Tablespoons Fructose sugar

Blend 30 seconds in blender.  Ready to serve.
Store in refrigerator

43

## SOUPS AND STEWS

### A QUICK STEW

Pour into a pan:
   1 can tomato soup
   1 can beef broth (Sold in grocery stores)
   1/2 cup red wine or burgandy

Do not heat yet. Blend in 3 Tablespoons flour, 1 teaspoon salt, dash pepper, and 1 Tablespoon basil. Add 1 1/2 pounds beef chuck cut into 1 inch cubes, 3 medium potatoes cut in half, 6 sliced medium carrots, and 1 large chunked onion.

Now heat at low temperature. Simmer 1 1/2 hours, stirring occasionally.

(You can cuddle on the couch with your sweetie while it's cooking.)

### POTATOPEA SOUP

*A Never-Fail recipe*

   4 large potatoes (unpeeled, of course)
   1 medium sweet white onion
   1 can (15 ounce) small sweet peas

Chunk the potatoes and onions. Put in pan, cover with water, and boil for 30 minutes.

Remove potatoes and onions from pan and blend in a blender until goupy and put them back in the pan.

Pour contents of can of peas in the blender and blend them with 1/8 cube of butter for 2 minutes.

Pour it into the pan with the potatoes and onions and cook for 10 minutes under medium heat.

It's ready to eat.

## FANTASTIC BURGANDY STEW

1 small can tomato sauce
2 Tablespoons beef soup base
2 cups water

Mix above well and add 1 cup Mountain Burgandy wine.

Blend in 3 Tablespoons stone ground whole wheat
flour, 1 teaspoon salt, 1/8 teaspoon pepper, and 1/2
teaspoon basil.

Cut 2 pounds beef chuck into cubes.

Cut 3 medium potatoes, 6 large carrots, and 1 large
onion into big chunks (Like a golfball).

Throw them in with the soup base and simmer for 1 1/2
hours, stirring occasionally.

## HAM AND PEA SOUP

4 15 ounce cans peas (drained, but save juice)
1 pound chopped ham
6 teaspoons corn starch
4 cups milk
2 small onions
1/4 pound butter (1 cube)

Boil ham and onions in 1/2 of the saved pea juice.
Mix the rest of the pea juice and all the other
ingredients in a blender or mixer. Put everything
together and cook for 15 to 20 minutes.

Do not get hot enough to scald the milk.

You're good to go.

## IMITATION CANNED VEGETABLE SOUP

1 15-oz can garbonzo beans
1 15-oz can or 28 oz can of green or string beans
1 15-oz can pea
1 15-oz can of stewed tomatoes
1 15-oz can whole kernel corn
1 15-oz can carrots or two large carrots, chopped
   into very little 1/4 inch cubes
2 medium size onions chopped into small chunks
1 15-oz can tomato sauce

Mix all above together in a 5 quart pan.

Boil one medium potato for 15 minutes then blend it
with its water in a blender until it turns into a mush.

Mix the mushed potatoes with the other ingredients in
the 5 quart pan and add:

1/4 teaspoon oregano
1/4 teaspoon marjoram
1/4 teaspoon sage
1/4 teaspoon thyme
1/8 teaspoon yellow curry powder

Bring to a boil. Remove from heat. It's ready to eat.

Uses:
It can be used as a delicious soup
it can be fried with hamburger as a casserole
it is great as a vegetable dish with almost any meal
it can be used in baked casseroles

The above recipe makes 3 to 4 quarts. You can store in
a freezer or refrigerator.

47

Here's an interesting soup:

**SEASONING SOUP**

2 large potatoes cut in 1" square chunks
3 medium onions cut in small chunks
3 large carrots in small chunks
4 celery stalks cut in 1/4 inch thick slices
1 1/2 cups barley (Pearl Barley)
1 teaspoon salt
1 teaspoon garlic
1/4 teaspoon ground thyme
1/4 teaspoon peppermill ground black pepper
1/8 teaspoon sage
1/8 teaspoon rosemary leaves
1/8 teaspoon oregano
1/4 teaspoon ground nutmeg
1/4 teaspoon dill weed
1/4 teaspoon whole sweet basil leaves
1/4 teaspoon whole celery seed
1/4 teaspoon parsley flakes
1 Tablespoon chili powder
1 Tablespoon beef boullion
1-1/2 quarts water
3 15-ounce cans cream of mushroom soup

Mix all together and cook in a crock pot on High heat for
1-1/2 hours. (If you don't have a crock pot, then cook on
a stove with the water barely bubbling for 1-1/2 hours).

Stir occassionally (never let it quite boil). You can simmer
it for 4 hours if you prefer. It takes less watching, that
way.

It's great and ready to eat.

Freeze leftovers for later.

# HAM POTATO SOUP

*A Never-Fail Recipe*

Boil a 1 pound ham (frozen or thawed) in 2-1/2 quarts of water for 45 minutes. Make a batch of Hollandaise Sauce (Page 70) while the ham is boiling. Remove ham from water. Pour half the water in a second pan. Keep both pans of water. Boil 3 medium size chunked onions, and 3 medium size thinly sliced carrots, in half the water for 20 minutes.

In the other pan, boil 6 medium size chunked potatoes and one small bunch of leaf lettuce for 20 minutes.

Put the potatoes and lettuce in a blender and blend into a thick goup. (You'll have to turn the blender on to do this.)

Put the potato water, goup, and 1 cup of Hollandaise sauce with the carrots and onions.

Cut ham into very small cubes about 1/2 inch per side.

Bring the whole mess to a boil for 5 minutes stirring slowly.

Eat it, freeze it, or give it to your friends. It is a very fine thick or medium thick soup.

REMEMBER: Do not peel the potatoes. Always leave the skins on. Merely scrub them before using. This is important for good flavor.

How are you coming along, by now?

## A GOOD CUPBOARD STEW

Dump into a large pan:   (all 15 ounce cans)
　　1 can peas and juice
　　1 can green beans and juice
　　1 can stewed tomatoes and juice
　　1 can tomato soup
　　1 can cream of chicken soup
　　1 Tablespoon beef soup base
Any additional vegetable and/or meat juice
from the refrigerator
　　1 6-ounce can tomato paste
Chunk, then add to above, the following:
　　Turnips
　　rutabagas
　　cauliflower
　　celery
　　carrots
　　ham hotdogs
　　vienna sausage
　　Any kind of left over potatoes
Boil 30 minutes, stirring occasionally.  You now
have a perfectly one dish balanced meal.

## FANTASTIC BURGANDY STEW

1 small can tomato sauce
2 tablespoons beef soup base
2 cups water
1 cup mountain red burgandy wine
Mix all of the above well in a pan or crock pot, then blend in 3 tablespoons stone ground whole wheat flour, 1 teaspoon salt, 1/8 teaspoon pepper, and 1/2 teaspoon basil.

Cut two pounds of beef chuck into 1 inch cubes

Cut 3 medium size unpeeled potatoes (Never peel a potato - always leave the skins on) into large chunks. Do the same with 6 medium carrots and 1 large onion.

Simmer for 1-1/2 hours - stirring occasionally.

51

## ROAST STEW

2 pounds roast (any kind - beef)
4 large potatoes, unpeeled, cut in quarters
4 medium onions, cut in half
4 large celery sticks, cut in half

Put in roast pan, fill one-inch deep with water. (You can use last night's roast, if Herby didn't eat it.) Roast 1-1/2 hours at 350 degrees.

Remove from oven, let cool, cut everything into bite size chunks and put in pan with:

    4 more large potatoes, first boiled 20 minutes
    and mashed in a blender with 1/8 cube
    butter, until goupy.

Mix the whole batch together with a wooden spoon. Add enough water to cover everything if necessary. Add season if desired, but I don't season it at all.

Boil 10 minutes.

Eat it or freeze for posterity or later use.

It's delicious.

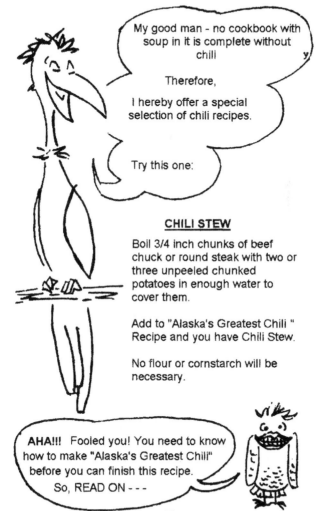

My good man - no cookbook with soup in it is complete without chili

Therefore,

I hereby offer a special selection of chili recipes.

Try this one:

### CHILI STEW

Boil 3/4 inch chunks of beef chuck or round steak with two or three unpeeled chunked potatoes in enough water to cover them.

Add to "Alaska's Greatest Chili " Recipe and you have Chili Stew.

No flour or cornstarch will be necessary.

AHA!!! Fooled you! You need to know how to make "Alaska's Greatest Chili" before you can finish this recipe.
So, READ ON - - -

## JUST PLAIN CHILI

1 lb fried hamburger
1 can dark red kidney beans
1 small chunked onion
1 6 - 8 oz can tomato sauce (For you mathematicians
    That's 1/2 of a standard 15 ounce can)
1 Tablespoon chili powder
3 Tablespoons chunked chili peppers
Enough water to cover the above.

Boil 30 minutes and eat.

## BURGANDY BEEF CHILI

Make a double recipe of Burgandy Beef Sauce (Page 71)

Simmer 2 lbs hamburger and 1 pound small chunks of chuck or sirloin roast in the sauce for 90 minutes.

After starting all of above simmering, add 2 large chopped onions, 2 rounded Tablespoons chili powder, 1/4 cup chopped hot chili peppers, 1 thin sliced carrot, 1 small can tomato paste, 2 cups water or vegetable juice left over from any previous cooking.

Lightly cover top of brew with garlic powder. Chop up one stalk of Bok Choy (an oriental green vegetable available in most super markets) and throw it in the pot.)

Stir occasionally while cooking.

(Bok Choy can be substituted by using one stalk of celery.)

By the way, chili is good both hot and cold!!!

**And here's the one you've been waiting for!!!**
**The Fantastic - - -**
## ALASKA'S GREATEST CHILI

Brown 2 lbs mooseburger or hamburger in a frying
pan, then transfer the meat to a large pot, and add
a chopped up baseball sized onion.

Dump in two 15-oz cans of stewed whole tomatoes,
each cut in half by you first. Dump in the juice also.

Dump in 2 or 3 15-ounce cans of Dark Red Kidney
Beans. Add 2 thinly sliced large carrots.

Chop 2 larges pieces of celery and 1/4 Green Bell
Pepper and chunk up one fresh tomato. (Guess
where they go) -That's right, in the pot also.

Add two rounded Tablespoons of Chili Powder and
1/8 cup finely chopped green, hot chili peppers,
including the seeds.

Add one or two 8-ounce cans of tomato paste .

Mix up the whole mess with a wooden spoon
and boil slowly for 30 minutes, stirring
occasionally.
Now eat it.

It can be frozen

(But it tastes better thawed and cooked.)

"Alaska's Greatest Chili" has received wide acclaim and praise as one of the best-tasting chili's known to mankind.

No matter how big a pot you make, it's not likely to last very long. Men will hike through raging snow blizzards, swim the Yukon river, snowshoe accross the tundra - - all for a bowl of "Alaska's Greatest Chili"!

And now, for those who count calories, here is:

### 242 CALORIES PER CUP CHILI

(Makes 4 cups)

16 ounces (1 pound) ground beef
15 ounce can dark red kidney beans
1 sliced medium carrot
1 chopped medium size onion
6 ounce (1 small can) tomato paste
1 Tablespoon hot chili powder
2 ounce (1/4 cup) hot chili powder

Pre Fry the ground beef. Next, mix everything together and cook 20 minutes at medium high heat, stirring occasionally.

# SALMON CHOWDER

*(King Salmon, Silver Salmon, Red Salmon, etc)*

Slice the back of a cleaned fish from end to end clear to the bone. Bake in a 350 degree oven for 1-1/2 hours over strips of bacon. Cut 3 doorknob size potatoes and 2 small onions into 8 chunks each and boil 15 minutes.

Chop 3 more potatoes and 2 onions into thumbnail size pieces, put in 5 quart pan, cover with water, and boil for 15 minutes.

Cut 6 bacon slices down the middle lengthwise. Then cut them crosswise into thumbnail size pieces. Fry these on high heat for 2 minutes. Put them on a napkin on a small plate to be added to the chowder later.

Blend the first group of potatoes, onions, and boiling water and pour into a blender and blend into a mush. Put the mush, 2 10-oz cans tomato soup, 1 15-oz can cream style corn, and the bacon bits in the pan with the other potatoes and onions. Add 2 tomato cans full of milk, (just the milk, throw the cans away), into the 5 quart pot. Add 1 teaspoon Garlic Powder, 6 teaspoons salt, 1 teaspoon Pepper, 1/2 teaspoon curry powder. and 2 teaspoons sugar.

After the fish has baked for 1-1/2 hours, remove the meat fom the bones and the skin, and put in the 5 quart pot. Take the bacon strips from the baking pan and cut them into small pieces, like you did the other bacon, and throw them into the pot.

Heat and stir for 15 minutes.

This stuff tastes really good!

## BREAKFAST RECIPES

1. Cold Cereal

2. Scrambled Eggs

3. Scrambled Ham and Eggs

4. Fried Eggs in Butter

5. Hard Boiled Eggs

6. Fried Eggs and Potatoes

7. Poached Eggs

8. Eggs "McMuller"

9. The Fantastic Eggs Benedict
   (Everybody's Favorite)

## 1. COLD CEREAL

By far the easiest. Pour your choice of cereal, such as corn flakes or whatever, into a bowl. Sprinkle a teaspoon of sugar over it, if it isn't sugar coated. Poor some milk over it and eat it - (use a spoon). Tastes good with pieces of fruit in it also. (Fresh or canned fruit pieces.)

## 2. SCRAMBLED EGGS

Pour a Tablespoon of vegetable oil into a frying pan of about medium size. (8" to 10" diameter). (If you need to, get a ruler and measure the width of the pan.) Wipe the oil around the pan with a paper towel.

Now crack 3 eggs, one at a time, against the edge of the sink just hard enough to crack the shell. Hold the eggs over a bowl, one at a time, and pull the shells apart so the eggs fall in the bowl. Pick the shell pieces that fell in, from the bowl.

Pour the eggs from the bowl into the pan, add two tablespoons of milk, break the yolks, and stir it up with a fork. Cook on medium low heat (#3 on the burner dial) while turning over and over with a spatula.
Good eggs take a little practice. Now go for it!

Next time, I'll use the fork, like the recipe says.

Now turn a stove burner to medium-high heat and place the frying pan on the burner.

As the eggs are cooking, stir them continuously with a spatula.

SPATULA

As you are stirring them, continuously scrape them from the frying pan bottom and turn them over. This will keep them well mixed, and will also keep them from sticking to the bottom and burning,

When they look like they are cooked solid, and are not runny, then they are done.
SO EAT THEM!!

NOTE:
Cooking eggs takes more care than other foods and will take a little practice. Don't be alarmed or upset if you don't do real well the first time.

Some people liked their eggs a little softer than others, with the yolks and/or whites almost a little runny. That's up to the individual taste.
Scrambled eggs are the easiest to learn and practice (other than hard-boiled eggs).

## 3. SCRAMBLED HAM AND EGGS

Cut up a piece of ham into small chunks, the size of your little fingernail. The easiest way to do to this is to cut a slice of ham about 1/4 inch thick first (that's about the thickness of a car door window). Then cut it into the smaller chunks.

**HAM**

SLICE

Now cut the ham slice crosswise and length wise and you now have a bunch of little square chunks.

Mix them in a bowl with 3 eggs and 2 Tablespoons of milk and scramble the whole mess just like the second recipe.

To add some flavor, you can add a teaspoon of onion salt to the mess before you begin cooking it, and mix it up real good.

## 4. FRIED EGGS IN BUTTER

Place the frying pan on a burner and turn the heat to medium.

Now spread about 1/2 cube of butter all over the pans inner surface. The butter will slowly melt as the pan gets hot. Spread it with a spatula so you won't burn yourself.

Always keep cold water handy, so if you burn your fingers or claws, you can stick them in cold water to cool them down. That's the best burn treatment.

Whenever cooking with butter, don't let butter burn. If it gets too hot and foamy and bubbly, then turn the heat down a little bit.

(Now on to the next page.)

Now, carefully crack an egg shell and hold it over the frying pan, close to the surface of the pan. Separate the shell so that the egg falls into the pan without breaking the egg yoke.

Now let it cook until the white of the egg turns solid white in color and is no longer runny.

Next, carefully slide the spatula under the egg, lift the egg with the spatula, and turn it over in the pan. Let it cook exactly 15 seconds.
You now have an "over easy" egg, ready to eat.

With practice, you can cook several eggs at the same time, in the same pan. If they stick together, then cut them apart with the front edge of the spatula before turning them over.

## "SEPARATING EGG YOLKS FROM EGG WHITES"

Pour yolks from one egg shell into the other and the whites will fall out into the bowl as shown below. (some times you need only the whites or only the yolks)

**Remember this technique !!!**

## CAUTION

You shouldn't flip eggs at first with the frying pan.

However, I suppose you're going to want to show off to your sweetheart.

When you finally do show her, have her stand back, out of the way. It's easier on her hairdo that way.
(And your shins.)

WATCH
OUT
FOR
FALLING
EGGS

## 5. HARD BOILED EGGS

Place the eggs, still in their unbroken shell, in a pan. Pour in enough water to completely cover them.

Boil them for 10 - 12 minutes. Then remove them from the heat, cover the pan with a lid, and let sit for 10 minutes. This will cook both the whites and the yolks.

If you cook them only 5 minutes, then you will have:

## 6. SOFT BOILED EGGS

The whites will be cooked solid, but the yolks will be soft and/or runny, and you'll be in for a surprise when you crack them open.

It could be a little messy if you crack them open expecting a hard yolk, but get a runny one.

Of course, if you only cook them for a minute:

## 6. FRIED EGGS AND POTATOES

First, cut up a potato about the size of your fist into pieces about the size of a dice. Or, cut the potato in half lengthwise, then cut each half into two pieces lengthwise.

Then slice the pieces, one at a time, crosswise into about 1/4 inch thick slices. (Use a ruler to measure the thickness, if you want).

Smear a little vegetable oil around a frying pan. Put it on a burner and turn the heat to high and fry the potatoes for 10 - 15 minutes, turning them over regularly with a spatula. Turn heat down if necessary, to keep them from burning.

They are done when you can stick a fork into them and they won't break. (They soften as they cook.)

Now, fry some eggs as in recipe number 4 (Page 62) and you have potatoes and eggs. Onion salt or chopped onions mixed with the potatoes add flavor.

When frying eggs, you can use vegetable oil or bacon grease instead of butter, if you want.

## 7. POACHED EGGS

Poached eggs are usually cooked in a special pan
which cooks them          with steam .

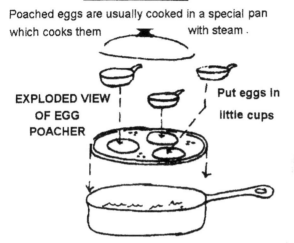

EXPLODED VIEW
OF EGG
POACHER

Put eggs in
little cups

The water boils, turning to steam, which rises up and
cooks the eggs. It only takes 1 to 3 minutes to poach
an egg.

You want the whites to be hard and the yolks to still
be soft. It'll take a little practice to get what you want.

Poached eggs are real good when served on a piece of
toast, with fried potatoes, or even by themselves.

And you'll want poached eggs for the famous Eggs
Benedict. That recipe is coming up after the next one.

## 8. EGGS "McMULLER"

Separate an English Muffin and place the two halves in oven under the broiler with a slice of American Cheese over one half.
Turn the broiler on. (It cooks better, that way.)
Now put an egg in a frying pan, break the yolk and mix it with the white and fry over medium heat until it is cooked solid.
Now turn off the broiler and the burner. Put the egg over the cheese and the other half muffin on top of the egg.
You got it!

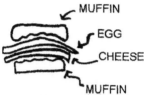

MUFFIN
EGG
CHEESE
MUFFIN

You can also make this by putting a ham slice over one half the muffin, cheese over the other half, broiling them while frying the egg. The results are fantastic.

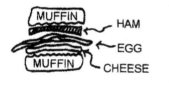

MUFFIN
HAM
EGG
MUFFIN
CHEESE

## 9. EGGS BENEDICT

You need:
   One half of an English Muffin
   One slice of ham
   One Poached Egg

   Hollandaise Sauce to pour over the top

POACHED EGG

HAM SLICE

   The Ham and Muffin taste better if heated under broiler for 3 to 5 minutes. A toaster oven can do this also.

   And now for Hollandaise and other sauces --

Where's that other egg? I know I had it here somewhere!

Hee
Hee
Hee

## AN EASY HOLLAINDAISE SAUCE

*A Never-Fail recipe*

Makes 1 1/2 to 2 cups

2 Tablespoons or 1/2 cube soft REAL butter
3 egg yolks (See Page 63 for separating Yolks)
2 teaspoons cornstarch
1-1/2 Tablespoons lemon juice
1/2 teaspoon salt
1/4 teaspoon paprika

Put all six items in a blender and blend until it becomes a thick cream.

Pour in one cup of boiling water and blend well. (It'll be thinner this time).

Put into a double boiler (pan inside a pan with boiling water in the larger pan) and stir until thick. (to make it thinner, add a little milk).

(A regular pan can be used if you use VERY LOW HEAT.)

**DOUBLE BOILER**

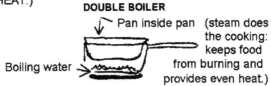

Pan inside pan (steam does the cooking: keeps food from burning and provides even heat.)

Boiling water

USES FOR HOLLANDAISE SAUCE:
1. Eggs Bebedict
2. Pour over Fried Eggs
3. Any other eggs
4. Topping for vegetables
5. Add to soups and stews for fantastic flavor
6. Topping for meats (Steaks or Roast slices)
7. Flavoring for groovy gravy

The following miscellaneous sauces have many uses. I'm putting them all under sauces for easy future references.

## BURGANDY BEEF SAUCE

1 can tomato soup
1 cup water
2 Tablespoons stone ground whole wheat flour
3 Tablespoons beef boullion
1/2 cup red burgandy wine
1 teaspoon salt
A dash of pepper (Dash  means "A Tiny Bit")
1 chopped large oniion

Mix up good and simmer on low heat for 30 minutes.

USES FOR BURGANDY BEEF SAUCE:

1. Cover vegetables, potatoes, and/or meat
2. Soup Base (See Chilis)
3. With beef appetizers

## BOB'S BARBRCUE SAUCE

Mix the following ingredients together in a pan.

1 1/2 cups tomato catsup
1/2 cup vinegar
1/2 cup lemon juice
1 Tablespoon regular sugar
3 rounded Tablespoons brown powdered sugar
2 teaspoons chili powder
1/4 teaspoon salt
1 Tablespoon Worcestershire sauce

Cover top lightly with 1/2 teaspoon black pepper.

Heat over menium heat while stirring until hot.

It's ready. Pour over steak, spare ribs, fish, etc.

Optional ingredient: 2 Tablespoons Taco sauce.

If thicker sauce is desired, add 1 ten ounce can of tomato puree or 1 six ounce can of tomato paste.

Makes approximately 18 to 20 ounces without the puree or paste. (16 ounces would be one pint and 32 ounces would be one quart.)

PSSST---
The Sweet Lime is
my favorite!

72

## BOB'S SWEET LIME BARBECUE SAUCE

1-1/2 cups tomato catsup or ketchup
1/2 cup white vinegar
1 Tablespoon Worcestershire sauce
1/2 cup lime juice
3 heaping Tablespoons brown sugar
3 rounded teaspoons hot chili powder
1/2 teaspoon salt and 1/2 teaspoon pepper
1/4 teaspoon onion powder

Blend well (that means stir up real good).
Heat slowly in a sauce pan and serve.
Makes approximately 1 quart.

It's real sticky, so try
not to slop it on the
deck. (A deck is a
floor)

73

## PEACH SAUCE

For Hams, Yams, and Pork

1/4 cup liquid brown sugar (1/4 cup powdered brown
    sugar dissolved in 1/4 cup hot water)
1/4 teaspoon salt
1/2 cube butter
1/2 teaspoon cinnamon

Heat until it boils, then add peach syrup from a 1 pound can
of peaches. (The syrup is the peach juice in the can, in case
you're wondering.)

Remove it from the heat, stir it up, and it's ready for use.

## SWEET SAUCE - CANDY SAUCE

(For Yams, Candied Sweet Potatoes, etc. - excellent for
squash)

Melt slowly one cube of butter. Then add:
    1-1/2 cups brown sugar
    1 capful Vanilla extract (That's cApful not cUpful.)
    1 capful maple extract  (Same as above, one cApful.)

Stir slowly while heating until it begins to bubble, then
remove fom heat.

For squash, yams, spuds ("spuds" is a highly technical
name for "potatoes", used commonly amongst bachelor
cooks.)

Pour the sauce over any of the above and bake at 300
degrees for 10 - 15 minutes.

## EXTRA SHARP THICK CHEDDAR CHEESE SAUCE

Blend one large boiled potato in blender with 1/4
cup water. This should produce potato mush. (I call
it "Mushed Potatoes").
Melt 1/2 to one cube butter in a saucepan and add
the "Mushed Potatoes" in also.
Add 1-1/2 cups milk, and heat the pan while stirring.
When the milk is hot, add 1 pound of grated extra
sharp cheddar cheese and 1/2 teaspoon salt. Mix
thoroughly until the cheese is melted. Mix for 3
minutes more. (It's a good arm excercise, too).

Uses: Pour over potatoes and bake. Pour over eggs.
Pour over baked fish. Pour over veggies, etc.
Use for soup as is or as a soup base.

It's best to wear a bib or
apron, or at least cover your
lap with a napkin when
eating sauces.

## MUSHROOM SAUCE #1

1 4-ounce can mushroom stems
1 10-3/4 ounce can cream of mushroom soup
1 rounded teaspoon of beef boullion or beef soup
    base

Put the three ingredients together in a small skillet or saucepan and cook at medium heat while srirring until hot.   It is ready to serve.

Very good over broiled steaks. (No extra seasoning is required.)

NOTE:
It might taste somewhat salty when cooling. Don't let it bother you.  Just cook it and serve it.

## MUSHROOM SAUCE #2

1 10-3/4 ounce can of mushroom soup
1 teaspoon "Kitchen Bouquet for Meat and Gravy"
1/8 cup milk
3 shakes of garlic salt - in other words, just a little bit
1 teaspoon beef boullion (Preferably the quick
    dissolve kind - it says so on the label.)
1-1/2 Tablespoon Soy Sauce

Mix it all up in a pan.

Heat until hot - while stirring.

Use for gravy, meat sauce, and/or vegetable sauce.

Also good for soup flavoring.

## SHARP CHEDDAR CHEESE SPREAD

2 lbs grated sharp cheddar cheese
1 lb Philadelphia Cream Cheese
2 teaspoons hot chili powder
12 finely chopped hot chili peppers (with seeds)
1 Tablespoon fresh milk
Mix all together in a bowl or pan. For best results use a double boiler to keep cheese warm and workable. Stir everything until the two cheeses are well blended together. (Serve at room temperature).
Good with crackers, sausage, ham, and as sandwich spread.
(For a milder, softer spread, add an extra 8 oz of cream cheese)

## MEATBALLS: BEEF AND PORK

1 pound Ground beef or hamburger
1/2 pound pork pattie sausage or ground pork
1 cup crushed crackers (any kind will do), saltines
and/or wheat thins are good.
A general rule is 2 parts ground beef, 1 part ground
pork, and 1/4 part crushed crackers. Put in pan and
sprinkle the top with black pepper, onion salt, sage, and
oregano. (Same amount of each- enough to lightly cover
the top of the mixture). Mix well with your CLEAN
fingers.
Form into 1 inch diameter balls and fry, bake, or freeze.
You can cook them from the freezer directly into the
oven and bake at 400 degrees for 30 minutes.
When cooked you can add them to spaghetti sauce,
gravy, mushroom soup, or any way you might like them.
They taste great.

---

When I make these meatballs, I make them with 5 lbs of
country style pork sausage and 10 lbs of ground beef so
I have 15 pounds of meatballs when I'm done. I freeze
them and they last 6 months to a year. This large a batch
takes about 2 hours to make.
Get your girl friend to help you roll them into balls.
Use your kitchen table with wax paper over it. You'll
need some room. A huge stainless steel or plastic bowl
is good for things like this.
Freeze them in wax paper 9 at a time with each package
wrapped in food film.

78

## BAKED MEATBALLS

Dig 18 meatballs out of your freezer.

Slice 3 small or medium potatoes lengthwise once, then crosswise into thin slices. Do the same with 2 small onions.

Put all the above well mixed together in a baking dish and cover the top with sage and salt. Mix it up again.

Mix 1 cup of sifted stone ground flour into 3 cups of milk.

Pour the milk and flour into the baking dish with the meatballs, potatoes, and onions.

Bake 1-1/2 hours at 325 degrees.

Delicious!

## MACARONI AND MEATBALLS

Buy 2 packages of macaroni and cheese. The cheese is in a little packet inside the box. Put it aside.

6 cups boiling water
1/2 pound chunked cheddar cheese
1/2 cube real butter
3 packages (9 per package) meatballs from your freezer.

Put the packages of macaroni and all the above ingredients into the boiling water. Boil for 20 minutes while stirring.

Add the two packages of cheese and 1 Tablespoon of salt. Cook while stirring for 5 minutes.

Now eat it.

## HAMBURGER HASH

1 lb hamburger or ground beef
1 large onion
2 large potatoes

Grate the onions and potatoes into thin long strings.
It's OK if the onions fall apart into little chunks.

Mix everything together with a little salt and fry in a
cast iron skillet until done. (Doesn't have to be cast
iron, there's no law against using any kind of skillet
your little heart desires.)

This is excellent with poached eggs or fried eggs with
runny yokes.

## CORNED BEEF HASH

2 lbs corned beef
6 strips bacon (if desired)

Put above through a meat grinder with medium teeth.

Dice in very small potato cubes. Amount of potatoes = 2/3
the amount of ground meat. Then dice one medium onion

in very small                          cubes.

Actual size >>>                         for potatoes and onions.

Mix everything together well with your CLEAN fingers.
You now have Corned Beef Hash. You can fry it, bake it,
put eggs in it - anything you want as long as you cook it.

Refigerate or freeze to store it.

Frying for ten minutes is perfect. Real good with
poached or fried eggs over the top or mixed in it.
Use as or in meatloaf, also.

And now for several boring pages of
good easy casseroles.

## BEEF AND MACARONI CASSEROLE

1 or 2 lbs frozen ground beef
3 packages meatballs
2 7-oz packages maceroni with the cheese included
1 Tablespoon onion salt
1 Tablespoon garlic salt
1 teaspoon black pepper
6 cups boiling water

Place hamburger in boiling water until it breaks apart,
then add everything else. Boil 20 minutes. The
meatballs can be boiled first with the hamburger.
(Break the hamburger apart with a spatula as it
thaws.)

## MR. AND MRS. MULLER'S MAGNIFICENT MILDLY MARVELOUS MOOSEMEAT CASSEROLE

### (Baked in an oven)

1 lb mooseburger
1/2 large can of pieces (Drained, but save juice)
1 diced boiled potato
1/2 chunked small onion
2 cups cooked elbow macaroni noodles
1 package brown gravy mix made with the pea juice
10 shakes Italian seaoning
6 shakes paprika
4 shakes dill weed
8 shakes ground oregano

Lightly cover with onion salt and garlic salt. Mix all
together in a casserole dish, bake at 350 degrees for 1
hour. (Add slices of American Cheese for last 20
minutes of cooking)

M-M-M-M-M-GOOD! per Judy Ann

## BAKED PORK CHOP POTATO CASSEROLE

3 or 4 unpeeled potatoes, thin sliced crosswise
2 pork chops
Flour (Any kind will do)
Cheddar or american cheese
Sage
1 small chopped onion
1/4 cube real butter
Grease with butter. Use a paper towel to cover the
baking dish bottom and sides. Cover dish bottom
with a layer of potato slices. Cover potatoes with
sage, flour, and onion chunks. Lay thin slices of
cheese on it.
Lay in one pork chop and cover it with potato slices.
Then sage, flour, onion chunks, and more cheese.
Lay in second pork chop and cover again with potato
slices, sage, flour, onion chunks, and more cheese.
Now pour milk into the dish until everything is
covered with milk.

Bake in oven at 350 degrees for 1-1/2 hours in
covered dish.

Absolutely delicious!

_____

## QUICK CASSEROLE

1 lb ground beef
1 or 2 unpeeled chopped potatoes
1 chopped onion
Fry all above with medium high heat - mixing with
spatula as they're cooking. When meat is cooked,
pour one 15 ounce can of creamed corn over the top
of it all and simmer a few minutes to heat the corn.
(I also like a drained 15 ounce can of peas poured in
with the corn.)

84

## HOT HAMBURGER SALAD

Fry in a skillet:
    1 stick sliced celery
    1 chunked small onion
    1 sliced unpeeled medium potato
    1 lb hamburger
    1/6 cube of butter
Mix with spatula while frying on high heat, When
cooked add:
    a 2 inch long piece of cucumber cut into small
    chunks
    1/4 bell pepper - chunked

Cover entire skillet with sage, pepper, and salt, then mix
all with a spatula while frying 3 to 5 minutes at medium
high heat.

For BEST RESULTS: Put seasonings in with all the
other ingredients at the very beginning.

## ITALIAN VEGETABLE CASSEROLE

4 links of Italian sausage - sliced
1 unpeeled potato - chunked
1 large onion
1 cucumber
1 Zuchini squash
1/2 fresh cauliflower
1 bell pepper
1 sliced large carrot
2 tomatoes
4 sticks celery
Burgundy or other red wine
Olive oil or vegetable oil
Lightly oil skillet and fry sausage and potatoes 5
minutes at high heat. Lower heat to medium high
and sloppily chunk all the veggies and throw them in
the skillet. Fill skillet 1/2 inch deep with wine and fry
3 - 5 minutes turning frequently. Serve while hot.
Leftovers make good soup or stew.

## BAKE PORK AND BEEF POTATO CASSEROLE

2 medium potatoes cut in half lengthwise and
   sliced into thin slices
1 large carrot, thinly sliced
2 chopped medium onions
2 pork chops - remove bones and cut into bite size
   pieces
1 pound stew meat (bite size pieces of beef)
9 pork and beef meatballs (page 78)
Mix the all the above together with your fingers. Now
cover the baking dish bottom lightly with flour.

Next put 1/2 of the mixed ingredients in the bowl and
cover them lightly with flour. Sprinkle sage, oregano,
thyme, curry powder, black pepper, and salt over the
top.

Put the rest of the mixed ingredients in the bowl over
the first layer and sprinkle the top with the same
seasonings.

Cover the top with 4 slices of American cheese cut into
little squares. Square size isn't particularly important.

Fill the baking dish with milk almost to the top. Cover
and put into a preheated oven at 350 degrees Bake
120 minutes and eat. (120 minutes is 2 hours.)

NOTE: If you're using frozen meat, all the meat can be
taken from the freezer and placed in hot tap water
("tap" means faucet) while you are cutting all the
veggies up and preheating the oven.

The meat will then be soft enough to cut into bite size
pieces when you are through cutting up the veggies.
(By the way, Meat cuts easier when partially frozen.)

## SPUDPEA RUMP ROAST CASSEROLE

1 cup elbow macaroni
1 lb beef rump roast cut in 3/4 inch thick slices
1/2 large white onion chopped in small pieces
1 15-oz can sweet peas, drained, (save the juice)
3 medium potatoes - cut in large chunks

Boil macaroni for 15 minutes in 3 cups water with 1 teaspoon salt.

In another pan boil the potatoes and onions with 1 tablespoon onion salt and 1 tablespoon pepper in enough water to cover them by 1/2 inch for 15 minutes.

At same time, cover meat slices with garlic salt and BROIL them 10 minutes on each side.

Now pour the potatoes and onions and their water in a blender and blend until you have a thick goup.

Cut meat into 1/2 inch square chunks.

Mix everything together and cook over a medium heat for 15 minutes. It's ready to eat.

You can refrigerate left overs, if there are any.

If you saved the pea juice, you can now add some of it to the refrigerated left overs and reheat. Stir while reheating or you'll burn some of the stuff on the bottom of the pan or skillet and the burnt smell will impregnate the rest of the food. (Your girl friend will not have been as impressed as she should have been.)

GOOD LUCK

Keep a cool kitchen tool, and don't forget to tell her: "You're the greatest cook in the world and I wish I could do better for you!"

Meatloaf Is an all time favorite. Here's a few recipes.

## SMALL HAMBURGER MEATLOAF

8 to 12 onces of hamburger or ground beef
1 small chopped up onion
1 bread heel (end piece crust) torn into small pieces
1/4 cup canned peas (no juice)
1/4 teaspoon thyme
1/4 teaspoon sage
1/4 teaspoon marjoram leaves
1/4 teaspoon ground black pepper

Mix up the whole mess well with your CLEAN fingers.

Put it all into an oiled pan.

Cover the pan with aluminum foil and stab the foil 4 times with a fork to provide ventilation.

Put in a cold oven and turn the oven button on to the 350 degrees setting. Cook for 2 hours or set the oven to 375 degrees and cook for 1-1/2 hours.

It is ready.

To be fancy, after one hour of cooking, cover the top with 1/2 can of cream of mushroom soup.

To be fancier, put some cut mushrooms in the soup before pouring it over the meatloaf.

Have fun!

89

## PORK AND BEEF MEATLOAF

1-1/2 pound ground beef
2 pork chops, bone removed and meat ground up
1 small chopped onion
1/4 to 1/2 bell pepper, chopped up
1 English muffin, dry and torn into crumbs or
    small chunks
1 teaspoon salt
1/4 teaspoon pepper
6 strips of bacon - ground or cut into very small
pieces


Mix the whole mess together with your fingers (CLEAN, of course) and put into a small baking dish. Cover the dish with a glass top. Bake at 350 degrees for 1 hour. (Read note at bottom of page.), then cover the meatloaf with 8 ounces (half a 15-oz can) of tomato sauce and bake for 30 minutes more with out glass top on the baking dish.
It is ready to eat. It can be eaten hot or cold and when sliced makes good sandwiches when used between two slices of bread. It tastes good by spreading mayonaise on a slice of it even without bread.

NOTE: Some meats may give out a lot of juice - if so, hold dish with a hot pan holder, and drain juice out before pouring on the tomato sauce. Also, you can buy squishy bulbs to remove the juice. They are available in grocery stores.   They suck the unwanted liquid out. I believe they are called "basters".


P.S.  I do hope you have been washing your hands before sticking your fingers in the food. If not - by all means do not tell your girl friend(s).

## REFRIGERATOR MEATLOAF

### (Absolutely NO seasoning)

1/2 to 1 lb hamburger
1/2 to 1 lb chopped up sausage pattie or links
1 piece chopped up left over ham - If available,
Up to 4 pieces of chopped up bacon - if available
Chopped up left over bell pepper
1 chopped up onion - small or large (Who cares?)
1 chopped up potato, any size, cooked or raw
1-1/2 to 2 ounces crushed crackers, any kind
1 piece of bread, torn into little pieces, dry or fresh,
    heal, crust or otherwise (No big deal)
1 or 2 pieces of celery, chopped

Mix everything together and put in an uncovered pan.

Cook at 350 to 400 degrees for one hour, then:

If you want, cover the top with any kind of cheese and bake an addional 5 minutes to melt the cheese.

(You can use sliced cheese, grated cheese, shredded cheese, powdered cheese, dehydrated cheese, just cheese.)

(You can use cheese sauce if you want.)

Sounds kinda cheesy, doesn't it?

Now eat it. .
Once, I kept track and I used the following recipe:

(Turn the page)

91

## "KEPT TRACK" REFRIGERATOR MEATLOAF

10 ounces ground beef (hamburger)
8 ounces pattie type pork sausage
1 2-ounce piece of fried ham, chopped up
1 medium boiled potato, chopped up
1 chopped up piece of celery
1 medium onion, chopped up
1/4 bell pepper, chopped up
1 soft bread crust (heel), torn into tiny bits
6 saltine crackers, finely crushed
6 sesame crackers, finely crushed

I mixed everything together with my clean fingers, while the oven was preheating to 400 degrees F, then put it all in a baking dish and mashed it to about 2 inches thick and put it uncovered in the oven for one hour.

Then I covered it with 3-1/2 ounces of sliced cheddar cheese and baked an additional 3 minutes.

My girl friend was so impressed with my cooking that she married me on 7 March 1980; and this meatloaf concocted from refrigerator leftovers on December 13, 1980, brought her highest praise.

Keep my "Kept-Track" recipe ingredients on hand. Use a 1 to 5 lb postal scale to measure everything, like I did. Cook it for your girl, and after she tells you that the food "trips the light fantastic" & "I'm madly in love with you, the world's greatest junk food cook", you can calmly say, "I just cleaned out the refrigerator. I'm glad you liked it."

## COMMENTS ON MEATLOAF:

You can cook it for one hour and then add cheese for five minutes, or add 1/2 can of mushroom soup or cover the top with 8 oz of tomato sauce and cook for an additional 10 minutes.

My honey says she likes meatloaf because there are so few dishes to wash afterwards.

Bell pepper and hamburger really go well together.

A chopped up carrot tastes good in meatloaf.

## AND SOME PARTY FAVORITES: APPETIZERS

## NACHOS

*A Never - Fail Recipe*

Cut flour or corn tortilla into triangles 2 inches accross top and 2 inches long. Cut Cheddar Cheese into the same shape and 1/8 to 1/4 inch thick.

Slice hot chili peppers into 1/4 by 1 inch pieces.

Slice green olives 1/8 to 1/4 inch thick.

Put pepper pieces on Tortilla pieces with olives on top of peppers and cheese over the olives slices.

Bake in 350 degree oven for 5 minutes (until cheese is melted).     Serve as is.

94

## BURGANDY BEEF CHUNKS

Make a double recipe of "Burgandy Beef Sauce" from page 71.

Cut chuck roast, sirloin roast or steak, round steak, etc., into 1 inch chunks. Use 2 lbs of beef per single recipe of Burgandy Beef Sauce.

Simmer all the above for 90 minutes. Serve in a crock pot or chafing dish to keep warm.

Or serve in little bowls or cups with cocktail forks.

People rave about this recipe.

Excellent for drinking parties. A little goes a long way. Make soup, stew, or chili from the leftovers. (If there are any.)

*** Either of these recipes can be served with toothpicks or small forks to pick the chunks out***

## COUNTRY STYLE BARBECUE BEEF CHUNKS

Cut country style beef ribs into 1 inch to 2 inch chunks and cover with barbecue sauce from Page 72 and 73 - barely covered.

Bake in 450 degree oven for 30 minutes. Serve in chafing dish to keep warm.

## FISH

A word about fish.

Fish must be cleaned. They can be baked whole.

They can be cut into fish steaks, which is cutting them crosswise:

STEAKS

They can be filleted. This means stripping or cutting the meat lengthwise away from the bones.

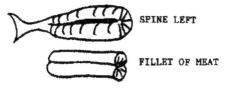

SPINE LEFT

FILLET OF MEAT

Fish steaks have bones, since you cut crosswise through both bones and meat.

Fish fillets have few or no bones.

With a whole baked fish, you can easily separate the meat from the bones and skin after it's been cooked.

("Whole" DOES mean "CLEANED".
NO GUTS ALLOWED!!!

# FISH

White Fish:    Haddock
                    Flounder
                    Sole
                    Ocean Perch
                    Grouper
                    Halibut

Cut into fillets or buy the fillets.

Lay in an oiled baking pan. Pour 1 15-oz can of
stewed tomatoes on them and bake at 350 degrees
for 30 minutes.

Delicious!

---

Cooking fish with tomatoes. tomato sauce, ketchup,
catsup, or other tomato products helps remove any
objectionable "Fishy smell or Fishy flavor".

Mayonalse smeared all over the fish before baking
helps also, however I much prefer the tomato method.
The flavor is better.

I often lay strips of uncooked bacon accross the
bottom of the baking pan and place the fish over the
bacon.
It tastes great and does not require greasing or oiling
the pan.
I mix tomato sauce or stewed, diced tomatoes with a
can of green beans and chopped onions over the fish
before baking.

(This works on every kind of fish I have ever cooked.)

## BAKED SALMON

King Salmon
Red Salmon
Silver Salmon
Atlantic Salmon

Cut off the head and tail. Clean out the guts. Pour stewed tomatoes in the cavity where the guts were. Slice a fresh tomato or 2 and a large onion and cover the salmon with them. Bake at 325 degrees for 1-1/2 hours for a small 6-8 lb fish. Two hours for a larger one. The fish is done when the inside meat is no longer translucent but is a solid color.

A large King, bake at 300 degrees for 3 hours. Some salmon approach a 100 lb weight and will take longer. Check the inside meat color occasionally.

## HALIBUT

Halibut is one of the finest tasting of all fish. It does not have a fishy taste.

It fillets easily and 90% of the fish is good meat.

Cheeks are considered a delicacy. A halibut less than 25 pounds is considered a "chicken halibut" and is a little sweeter than a larger one.

They grow more than 450 lbs, with the average between 25 and 75 pounds although Halibut over 100 pounds are fairly common.

Mix some beer and flour together into a paste, dip halibut chunks in it, and fry it. Tastes great!

It can also be cooked like any other fish.

## AN EASY HALIBUT RECIPE

1 cup flour (any kind, sifted)
2 eggs
1/4 cup baking powder
1/4 cup milk
1 teaspoon salt

Mix or blend above into a medium thick batter.

Add more milk if it is too thick.

Cut the halibut meat into 1 inch cubes or chunks or into long thin slices and dip in the batter.

Pour vegetable oil into a skillet about 3/4 inch deep. Heat vegetable oil at high heat. Reduce heat if it begins to smoke.

Cook halibut in oil until bottom is golden brown. Turn over and repeat.

It takes only 5 minutes or less for each side.

It is fantastic and can be used for dinner or for hors d'oeuvres ("Snacks" to the commoner).

It is good hot or cold and with or without sauce.
You can use Barbecue Sauce, hot mustard sauce, seafood sauce, honey, jam or jelly, or just about any sauce to dip it in that you like.

## SHRIMP

Frozen shrimp is easy to cook. (With shells on.)
Boil a quart of water with a tablespoon of salt in it.

Take the frozen shrimp - a whole pounds worth - and
drop it in the boiling water 5 minutes. When shells turn
pink, it is ready.

Place it over some lettuce leaves and serve it with
seafood sauce.

## ROCK LOBSTER

Rock lobsters are small and cook just like shrimp.

## CRAB

Frozen crab is also cooked just like shrimp.

## NOTE:

If you boil shrimp, lobster, or crab too long the
meat will get tough and not taste so good.

Remove the shell
first, Herby.

# DESSERTS

Here are 2 pie crusts. They require some work, but are worth it for apple pie, or most other pies for that matter.

If you make apple pie, then don't prebake the crust.

## LIGHT WHOLE WHEAT CRUST

(for a 10 inch diameter pie)
3 cups stone ground whole wheat flour
2 teaspoons salt
1 Tablespoon fructose sugar
3/4 cup cold 2% low-fat milk
1-1/2 cups canned vegetable shortening
Sift flour into a bowl. Add everything else. Squish everything together until well mixed with fingers. (By now it should be well imbedded in your mind to have CLEAN fingers.)

Cover a clean flat surface, such as a counter top, with sifted flour. Smash dough flat like a thin pancake by rolling a bottle or rolling pin over it. Place in a pie pan. There'll be enough left over for a top crust and a separate tart.
- For pre-baked crust, cook 10 minutes at 450 degrees -

*** HELPFUL HINT: If dough is too dry, wash hands in cold water, and, while wet - squish dough with fingers. The water from your hands will be absorbed by the dough, thus moisturizing it without making it too wet.

## HEAVY WHOLE WHEAT CRUST
(for a 10 inch diameter pie)

3 cups stone ground whole wheat flour
2 teaspoon salt
1 Tablespoon fructose sugar
3/4 cup cold 2% low-fat milk
1-1/2 cups vegetable oil
1/2 cup water

Sift flour into a bowl. Add everything else. Squish
everything together until well mixed with your, (Clean
of course), fingers.
Cover a clean flat surface, such as a counter top,
with sifted flour. Smash dough flat like a thin
pancake by rolling a bottle or rolling pin over it.
Place in a pie pan. There'll be enough left over for a
top crust and a serarate tart.
— For prebaked crusts, bake 10 minutes at 450
degrees —


*** HELPFUL HINT:
    If dough is too dry, wash hands in cold water
and, while wet, squish dough again with fingers.

The moisture from your hands will be absorbed by
the dough with out making it too wet or soggy or
goupy.

For a real "Never-Fail" recipe , use the Graham
Cracker or Vanilla Wafer crust on the next page.

It's especially perfect for Banana Cream pies.


104

## GRAHAM CRACKER OR VANILLA WAFER CRUST

Buy a box of round vanilla wafer cookies or square graham crackers.

Crush up 50 of them (either type) into fine crumbs with your hands or a rolling pin.

Now melt 1/4 cube of butter over medium heat and pour it in the crumbs.

Pour in 2 teaspoons liquid vegetable oil and 1/4 cup of regular granulated white sugar. Use a wooden spoon to mix everything up real well, crushing any large lumps into tiny ones.

When everything is well crushed and mixed up, then with your CLEAN hands, dump it all into a pie pan and spread it around evenly, both all over the bottom and up the sides of the pan.

Fill the pan with pie filling and bake. Or put the pan with the crumby stuff inside in the oven and bake at 375 degrees for 8 minutes.

Now you can remove it from the oven and fill with Banana Cream Pie filling (Page 106). Some people get real lazy and just lay the Vanilla wafer cookies accros the bottom and around the side of the pan.

You can do this if you want, but it tastes better and is more impressive for your sweetie if you make the crust and it only takes a few minutes to do.

## BANANA CREAM PIE

*A Never-Fail Recipe*

Prepare crust of your choice. Put it in a 10 inch pie pan and bake 10 minutes at 450 degrees. Remove from the oven, set on the counter, and let cool while you make the following banana custard:
Beat with an egg beater, blender, or mixer:
           5 egg yolks (See page 63)
Beat in slowly:  1/2 cup sugar
           1/2 cube soft or melted butter
           1/2 teaspoon salt
           3-1/2 Heaping Tablespoons Corn Starch
           2 teaspoons banana extract
Heat 4 cups milk in a pan until milk boils and begins to foam and rise up. Pour the hot milk into the above mixture and mix with a wooden spoon until thick. (The hot milk will cause the corn starch to thicken.)

Now cut 4 bananas (without the peels) into slices.

Cover the botton crust with banana slices. Pour custard over it. Lay in a second layer of banana slices and pour more custard over it. Keep adding more layers of bananas then custard until the pie pan is full of layers of banana slices and custard. Put in refrigerator until it is cold. Put whipped cream (page 108) over it and eat it.

FOR BEST RESULTS: Share with your girl friend— (Don't be a pig!)

------------------------

And throw your banana peels in the trash
Don't leave them laying around

------------------------

**G R R R R !**

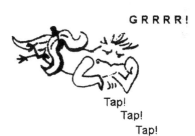

Tap!
Tap!
Tap!

## WHIPPED CREAM

You can buy all ready made whipped cream
or make your own

1 cup whipping cream ("whipping" not "whipped")
1 Tablespoon powdered white sugar
1/2 teaspoon vanilla extract

Put above in bowl and beat with an egg beater until
you have whipped cream.

You can buy all ready made whipped cream even
in spray cans.

AAWKK!

Thanks for the
banana peel,
Ralph.

## APPLE PIE

(Makes a 10 inch pie)

*(A Never-Fail Recipe)*

Prepare crust of your choice.

Peel 10 medium apples (for best results, have a girl peel the apple because guys waste to much apple)

Cut into medium slices length wise.

Put apple slices in a bowl.

Mix the following ingredients together then pour them over the apple slices:

    1 cup white granulated sugar
    4 heaping Tablespoons cornstarch
    1/4 teaspoon salt
    1/2 rounded teaspoon cinnamon
    1/4 teaspoon nutmeg

Mix very well with your CLEAN hands and fingers. Put it in a pie pan that has unbaked crust in it. Pile the apple mixture one inch higher than the edge of the pan as it will settle (shrink) somewhat when cooking.

Cover the top with crust also and poke some holes in the top to relieve steam pressure when it is cooking.

Cook 10 minutes at 450 degrees in the oven, then lower the temperature to 350 degrees and cook for 45 minutes more.

Eat hot or cold. Your sweetie might want a blob of ice cream on top of her piece. Vanilla ice cream goes well with apple pie.

## SO NOW YOU CAN COOK

Well, dress up and invite some unsuspecting lovely lady over for dinner. You now hold the world in your wings!!!

## NOTES ON FOOD SAFETY

FOOD POISONING is very common today. Bacteria grows between 41 degrees and 140 degrees F, so food should always be stored below 41 degrees and heated above 140 degrees, with some exceptions.

Meat can be cooked a little lower as long as it will be eaten right away. Bacteria does not grow inside the meat as it does on the surface. So the inside temperature can be below 140 degrees since the surface of the meat will be much hotter. Searing a steak before cooking it rare prevents bacteria from growing inside the meat.

Thaw food in the refrigerator, a microwave oven, defrost setting on an oven, or submerged in water in a covered container.

Buy a meat thermometer. One kind stays in the thickest part of the meat while cooking. Another kind you insert in the meat for a few minutes, when you want to check the internal temperature, then remove it.

Do not leave cooked meat out at room temperature for more than 2 hours. Otherwise bacteria will begin to grow on it.

All precooked meat must be reheated to an internal temperature of 165 degrees to be safe.

112

## TABLE OF MEASUREMENTS

Measures are important, but sometimes confusing.
So here are some of the ones you need to know:

### FLUIDS AND LOSE GRAINS (LIKE FLOUR)

1/2 ounce = 1 Tables spoon = 3 teaspoons
1 ounce ( abbreviated oz) = 2 Tablespoons
16 Tablespoons = 1 cup
8 ounces = 1 cup      2 cups = 1 pint
16 ounces = 1 pint      2 pints = 1 quart
32 ounces = 1 quart      4 quarts = 1 gallon
3 teaspoon = 1 Table spoon
1 Soup spoon = 2 teaspoons = 2/3 Tablespoon

### SOLIDS

16 ounces = 1 pound (abbreviated lb)

### BUTTER

Butter normally comes in 1 pound boxes (16 ounces).
1 Cube of butter is 1/4 pound, or 4 ounces, or
8 Tablespoons. So, 1 Tablespoon of butter is 1/8 cube
1 cube = 1/2 cup
2 cubes = 1 cup

### ALCOHOL

1 shot = 1-1/2 ounces = 45 ml = 3 Tablespoons
A 750 ml bottle holds 16-2/3 1-1/2 ounce shots or
   25 1-ounce short shots.
1.75 liter bottle holds 38.8 1-1/2 ounce shots or
   58.3 1-ounce short shots
1 quart = 1/4 gallon = 32 ounces = 964 ml = 0.964
   liters = 21.3 shots = 32 short shots
1 fifth =1/5 gallon = 25.6 ounces = 756.8 ml = 17 shots
   = 25-2/3 short shots

## ABOUT THE AUTHOR

He was born in Portland Oregon on 8 December 1941. His family moved to Seward, Alaska in 1943, where he was raised. When 13 years old, he was afflicted with Polio. After a few years of therapy he began running to strentghen his legs, lettering in track before graduating from Seward High School in 1960. The military sent him to Viet Nam after which he returned to Alaska to care for his mother who died shortly after his return.

He began a 37 year career in telecommunications with Alascom Inc, Alaska's first long distance company. ATT purchased Alascom in 1995, and in 2001, sent him to Georgia to their Global Switched Message Center to assist telephone companies around the world fix equipment problems via telephone. In Georgia, he was named "Alaska Bob" by his co-workers.

He quit ATT, because his legs were seriously impaired from the past and were getting worse. Returning to Anchorage, he began singing karaoke and soon became known again as "Alaska Bob" to differentiate him from other Bob,s. In 2008 and 2009 his hip bones were cut off and replaced with Titanium hips allowing him to walk without crutches and the life long pain of the past.

Throughout his life he has owned a restaurant, built a mobile restaurant, been certified as a FoodSafe employee, manager, and Instructor. He has been a member of ARBA and CHARR and attended bartender school obtaining a TPS bartender's certificate.

He holds over 150 Certificates in electronics, first aid, CPR, supervision, management, instruction, and other categories.

He is accomplished in many fields including mechanics, construction, electronics, and more.

He is publishing this book to show the world how easy cooking can be used to impress the ladies.